BARBRA STREISAND
HIGHER GROUND

Piano/Vocal Arrangements by John Nicholas
Photography: Front cover and this page, Randee St. Nicholas

Ms. Streisand's dedication and comments on the songs are reprinted from the Higher Ground CD booklet

Copyright © 1998 Cherry Lane Music Company
International Copyright Secured All Rights Reserved

The music, text, design and graphics in this publication are protected by copyright law. Any duplication or transmission, by any means, electronic, mechanical, photocopying, recording or otherwise, is an infringement of copyright.

 Visit our website at www.cherrylane.com

THIS SONGBOOK IS INSPIRED BY AND DEDICATED TO VIRGINIA CLINTON KELLEY.

On a January morning in 1994, I was one of hundreds of mourners at the funeral of Virginia Kelley, mother of President Clinton, professional spitfire, and a precious friend of mine. She had been a great role model for me, an angel on my shoulder, utterly unafraid to show unconditional love, kindness, and appreciation to everyone she met. Sitting there in that sanctuary of sadness, I heard many wonderful stories about Virginia, and beautiful songs sung in her memory. As the music filled the room, I felt my spirit moved to joy, my heart swelling with emotion. I knew Virginia was in safe hands, having a ball at the great racetrack in the sky.

At one point, a singer named Janice Sojstrand sang the opening lines of "On Holy Ground." It's hard for me to describe that electrifying moment. The music united us, invoking Virginia's essence and elevating our spirits with every note. I knew then that I had to sing that song, and others like it. The idea for this album was born at that moment.

When something tragic happens, whether it's Virginia Kelley's death, Princess Diana's, or that of anyone close to you, it wakes you up to the more important things in life. That's why I needed to sing these songs. Music is the connective tissue among souls. Moreover, I believe it is incumbent upon each of us to put positive thoughts out there in the universe, where they can be free to do their good work.

Firooz Zahedi

My plan was to sing a collection of songs that spoke to the hearts of all persons of faith. Certain familiar melodies—like "Kol Nidre" or "Silent Night"—were, I believe, inspired by God. And so, for this album, I sought songs that would inspire me (inspire: from the Latin, "to breathe in"). It's taken over three years, but finally, here we are with HIGHER GROUND. May these songs fill your soul with the breath of life and love and faith.

CONTENTS

- 8   I BELIEVE/YOU'LL NEVER WALK ALONE
- 16 HIGHER GROUND
- 21 TELL HIM
- 28 AT THE SAME TIME
- 34 ON HOLY GROUND
- 39 IF I COULD
- 43 CIRCLE
- 48 THE WATER IS WIDE/DEEP RIVER
- 56 LEADING WITH YOUR HEART
- 62 EVERYTHING MUST CHANGE
- 66 AVINU MALKEINU
- 72 LESSONS TO BE LEARNED

I BELIEVE/YOU'LL NEVER WALK ALONE

Beautiful melodies, beautiful thoughts. One was a hit for Frankie Laine in 1953, the other is from Rodgers & Hammerstein's "Carousel." Though both are familiar to most people, I heard "I Believe" as a classical tone poem. Both songs are simple stories about faith, and I wanted to revisit them in a less traditional way.

HIGHER GROUND

I wanted to call the album "Higher Ground" because it's a road I want to take myself. We've all seen how common it is for some people to tear others down, to diminish them and their accomplishments in order to feel better about themselves. The only way to fight back is to do good work and leave a legacy of some kind, one that is positive, uplifting, and, hopefully, motivating. When I first heard this song, I was told the writers had conceived the lyrics in a religious context. I thought it was a love song . . . but then again, aren't all religions about love?

AT THE SAME TIME

I adore the lyric of this song, which reflects exactly what I think: knowing how fragile the planet is, how fragile souls are, and how desperately we need unity. Look how the world came together after Princess Diana's death. We all saw how people need to be close, to love each other, to cry together, to feel together. I wish we could live like that all the time without having to wait for tragedy to strike.

TELL HIM
Duet with Celine Dion

Many years ago, my friend David Foster told me about a young singer from Canada named Celine Dion. He said she was really someone to watch. Over the years, I definitely did watch her, and I think she's absolutely fabulous. She has a kind heart and an amazing voice! As for the song, it's about an older (and hopefully wiser) woman advising a younger woman in love. I figure Virginia would have said, "Tell him . . . tell him you love him." It's better to err on the side of generosity when it comes to life and love.

ON HOLY GROUND

This is the song that started the whole project. I love the sound of a gospel choir, with all its earthy passion, so it was a real thrill for me to work with these fine singers. The lyrics say that whenever we stand in the presence of God, we're on holy ground. But since God is all around us, that would make every inch of this beautiful planet holy ground.

IF I COULD
For Jason

Sung from a parent to her child, "If I Could" meant a lot to me as a mother. It's about how we have to let go of our children eventually, something we moms and dads have a hard time doing. Though we wish we could, we can't protect them forever.

CIRCLE

It's been pointed out many times before, but it bears repeating: life is a circle. Generations of the past are mere dust, as we will be too someday. But love and faith endure.

THE WATER IS WIDE/DEEP RIVER

I first heard "Deep River" at age sixteen when I bought my first Johnny Mathis record at the supermarket for $1.98. He sang it so beautifully, the song always stayed with me. I thought it would be interesting to pair it with "The Water Is Wide." The two images, connecting "deep" and "crossing over" also resonate with me. I suppose we're all trying to get "to the other side," exist on a higher spiritual plane, one way or another.

LEADING WITH YOUR HEART

This song was a surprise! When my friends Marvin Hamlisch and Alan & Marilyn Bergman heard I was doing this album, they set out to write a song for it. They knew how much I loved Virginia Kelley, so they titled the song after her autobiography, <u>Leading</u> <u>With</u> <u>My</u> <u>Heart</u>.

LESSONS TO BE LEARNED

Though I always fight for the truth, I've had to accept the fact that there are negative forces out there that are quite strong. But the Bible says love is stronger than death, and so I continue to have faith that the truth will emerge eventually. This song explores that questioning side of faith, when we wonder why bad things have to happen to us. But in the end, the lessons we learn, from both the good and the bad, only strengthen our spiritual nature.

EVERYTHING MUST CHANGE

I first recorded this song in 1974, but I wasn't happy with the arrangement, so the song was shelved. Now 23 years later, I've come back to it. I love the pastoral quality of the melody, and how the lyric so succinctly describes the cycles of life. We all change, grow, age, and evolve. Learning to embrace that change, to celebrate it, is one of the most important lessons we'll ever learn.

AVINU MALKEINU

Sung during Rosh Ha'Shanah (the Jewish New Year), "Avinu Malkeinu" ("Our Father, Our King") is a supplication to God to treat us with kindness and generosity, even when we haven't always lived up to His ideals for us. The melody I sing here is so beautiful, surely the hand of God touched the composer.

(Translation)
Hear our prayer
We have sinned before Thee
Have compassion upon us and upon our children
Help us bring an end to pestilence, war, and famine
Cause all hate and oppression to vanish from the earth
Inscribe us for blessing in the Book Of Life
Let the new year be a good year for us

Avinu malkeinu sh'ma kolenu
Avinu malkeinu chatanu l'faneycha
Avinu malkeinu alkenu chamol aleynu
V'al olaleynu v'tapenu

Avinu malkeinu
Kaleh dever v'cherev v'raav mealeynu
Avinu malkeinu kalenchol tsar
Umastin mealeynu

Avinu malkeinu
Avinu malkeinu
Kotvenu b'sefer chayim tovim
Avinu malkeinu chadesh aleynu
Chadesh a leynu shanah tovah

Sh'ma kolenu
Sh'ma kolenu
Sh'ma kolenu

Avinu malkeinu

Avinu malkeinu
Chadesh a leynu

Shanah tovah

Avinu malkeinu
Sh'ma kolenu
Sh'ma kolenu
Sh'ma kolenu
Sh'ma kolenu

I Believe/You'll Never Walk Alone

I Believe
Words and Music by
Ervin Drake, Irvin Graham,
Jimmy Shirl and Al Stillman

You'll Never Walk Alone
Lyrics by Oscar Hammerstein II
Music by Richard Rodgers

I BELIEVE
Slowly, freely

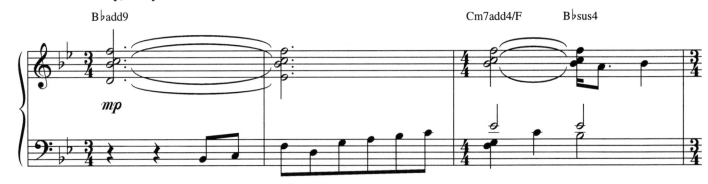

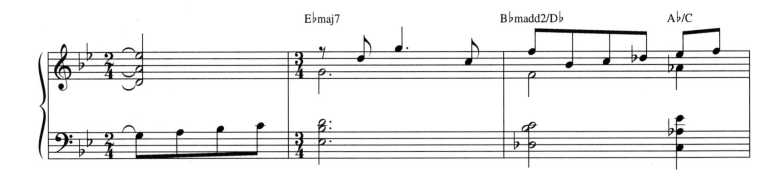

I Believe
TRO-©-Copyright 1952 (Renewed) 1953 (Renewed)
Hampshire House Publishing Corp., New York, New York
International Copyright Secured Made in U.S.A.
All Rights Reserved Including Public Performance For Profit
Used by Permission

You'll Never Walk Alone
Copyright © 1945 by WILLIAMSON MUSIC
Copyright Renewed
International Copyright Secured All Rights Reserved

Higher Ground

Words and Music by
George M. Green, Kent Agee
and Steve Dorff

Tell Him

Words and Music by
Linda Thompson, David Foster
and Walter Afanasieff

Copyright © 1997 Sony/ATV Tunes LLC, Wallyworld Music, One Four Three Music,
Warner-Tamerlane Publishing Corp. and Brandon Brody Music
All Rights on behalf of Sony/ATV Tunes LLC and Wallyworld Music Administered by
Sony/ATV Music Publishing, 8 Music Square West, Nashville, TN 37203
All Rights on behalf of One Four Three Music Administered by Peermusic Ltd.
All Rights on behalf of Brandon Brody Music
Administered by Warner-Tamerlane Publishing Corp.
International Copyright Secured All Rights Reserved

© 1997, 1998 WARNER-TAMERLANE PUBLISHING CORP., BRANDON BRODY MUSIC,
ONE FOUR THREE MUSIC and WALLYWORLD MUSIC
All Rights on behalf of BRANDON BRODY MUSIC
Administered by WARNER-TAMERLANE PUBLISHING CORP.
All Rights Reserved Used by Permission

At The Same Time

Words and Music by
Ann Hampton Callaway

*Recorded a half step lower.

ON HOLY GROUND

Words and Music by
Geron Davis

34

If I Could

Words and Music by
Ron Miller, Ken Hirsch
and Marti Sharron

CIRCLE

Words and Music by
Jud Friedman and Cynthia Weil

Slowly

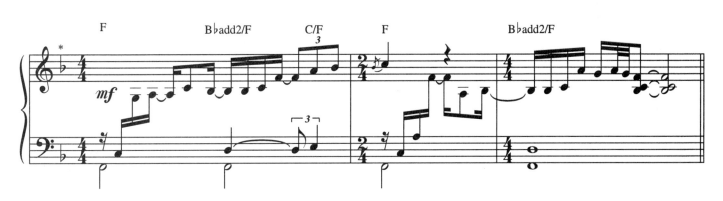

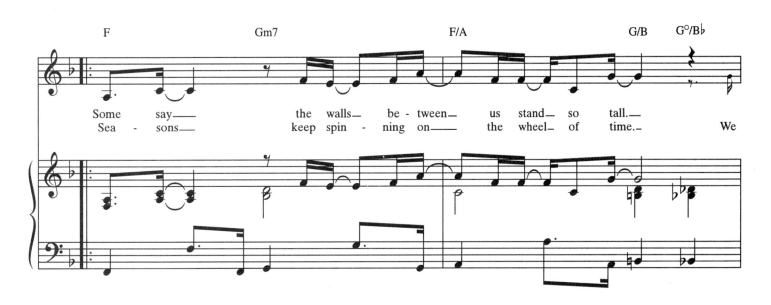

Some say— the walls— be-tween— us stand so tall.—
Sea-sons— keep spin-ning on— the wheel— of time.— We

They don't see— there's just one sun— shin-ing on us all.—
stand, we fall,— we strug-gle up— the moun-tains we— must climb.—

*Recorded a half step higher.

Copyright © 1997 by Peermusic Ltd., Schmoogie Tunes and Cynthia Weil Music
Copyright Renewed
All Rights for Schmoogie Tunes Administered by Peermusic Ltd.
International Copyright Secured All Rights Reserved

The Water Is Wide/Deep River

Traditional
Arranged by Arif Mardin

Leading With Your Heart

Words and Music by Marvin Hamlisch,
Marilyn and Alan Bergman

Everything Must Change

Words and Music by
Bernard Ighner

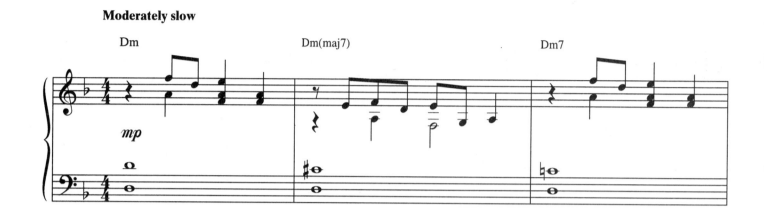
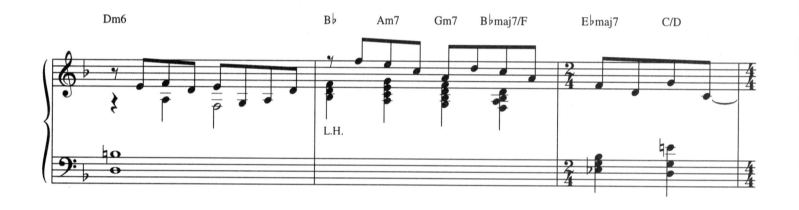
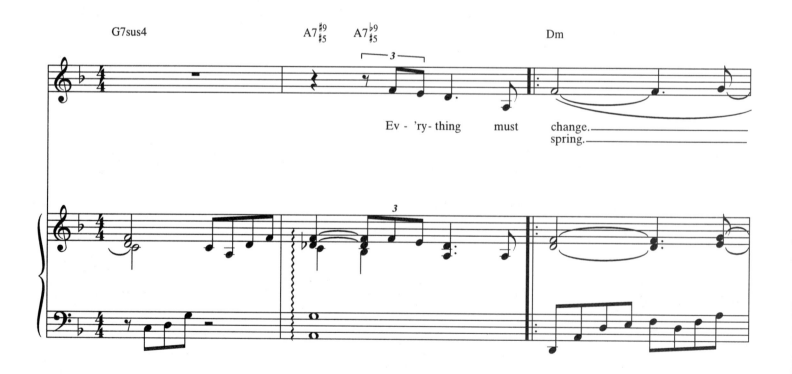

Ev-'ry-thing must change.
spring.

©1974 ALMO MUSIC CORP. (ASCAP)
All Rights Reserved Used by Permission

Avinu Malkeinu

Words and Music by
Max Janowski

Lessons To Be Learned

Words and Music by
Marsha Malamet, Alan Rich
and Dorothy Sea Gazeley

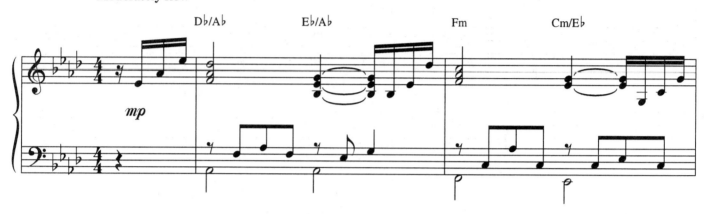

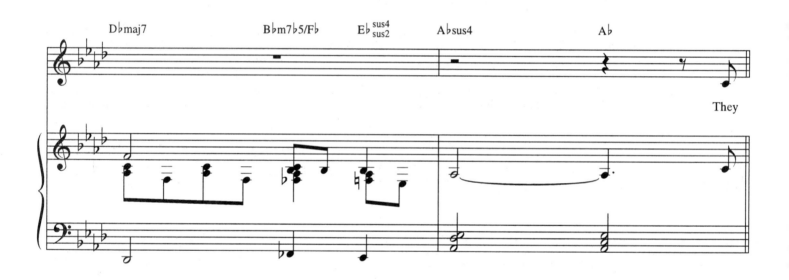

say, there's a u-ni-ver-sal plan for ev-'ry
up, keep on look-ing deep in-side. Let your

© Copyright 1997 NELANA MUSIC, MUSIC CORPORATION OF AMERICA, INC.,
GITSOMS SONGS, FAMOUS MUSIC CORPORATION and WRITE BY THE SEA MUSIC
All Rights for NELANA MUSIC Controlled and Administered by
MUSIC CORPORATION OF AMERICA, INC.
International Copyright Secured All Rights Reserved

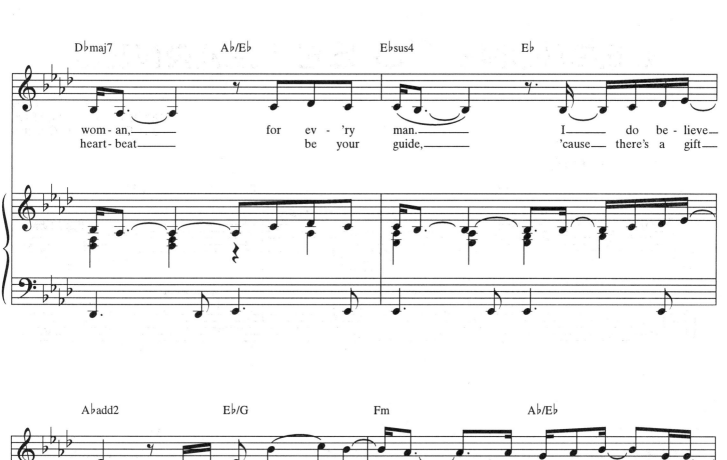

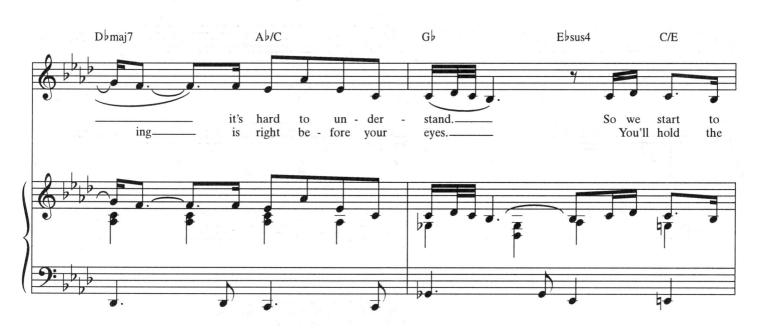

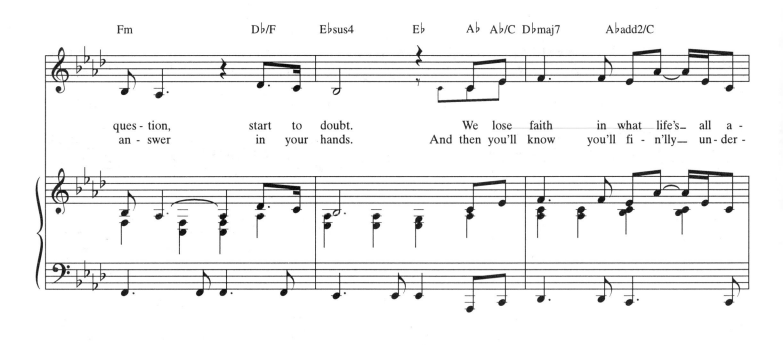